W0232731

VOLCANO

PRAISE FOR THE AUTHOR

'Eunice de Souza's poems have an accuracy of detail and something of the quality of photographs taken at a decisive moment—with individuals or groups fixed at their most acute moments of pretension, cruelty or loneliness—that make them memorable. The more introspective poems [are] no less sharply focused. In them the poet bears pain, however personal, not by the usual literary expediency of diffusing it but by mercilessly bringing it to light'—**Adil Jussawalla**

'*A Necklace of Skulls* is nothing less than the collected work of a pioneer . . . It will survive in the language of the mind, the vernacular in the deep sense, because that is the language in which she has, with unerring instinct, chosen to write it'—**Anjum Hasan,** *Caravan*

'If Kamala Das brought female sexuality into Indian verse, de Souza ushered in female rage—a white-hot, page-searing, bone-chilling fury'—**Arundhathi Subramaniam,** *The Hindu*

'What struck me at once about the poems was their immediacy, their complete impact, their unguarded sense of statement . . . There is a marvellous irony, delicately and at the same time savagely handled . . . I have been moved by these poems which have such directness, vigour and such a strange mixture of triumph, vision and agony'—**A.D. Hope**

'A master class in the art of brevity, Eunice de Souza's poems revel in savage humor and dazzling, epigrammatic punchlines. Short stanzas of seemingly unadorned speech offer both irony and tenderness, sometimes within the same sentence. Often imitated, never equaled, these gorgeous, combative, exceedingly wise lyric meditations serve as cultural histories and as maps to an extraordinary life. Finally available in a single definitive edition, here are poems to carry close, to memorize, poems that may change your mind and your life'—Jeet Thayil

'In these her late poems the volcano that is Eunice de Souza is still erupting. As in her early work too, what she here 'upchucks' is lava, molten lines that burn and glow and leave a permanent mark. The tone, as before, is casual, bantering, close to the spoken idiom that is uniquely hers. When terrible things happen the tone changes, quickens, then relaxes again. Life is bemusing, ludicrous; death even more so. In the work of no other poet I can think of do you find such brevity, grandeur, swiftness of utterance and the unbearable weight of grief, unbearable because de Souza is so dry-eyed. 'The crone's still capable/ of spite' she writes in one poem, the old necklace-of-skulls self-irony intact, except that in her case 'spite' also means 'wisdom'. It is easy to forget that the crone is deeply moral as well, and like any moral being she too feels that she's lived 'In the wrong season'. There is plenty in these spare but unsparing poems to remind us of the classical virtues we associate with Bhartrhari, for instance, or a Latin epigrammatist like Martial. These are poems to live by. In time, they will come to be seen as classics of our literature, as many of her earlier poems already are'—Arvind Krishna Mehrotra

VOLCANO

COLLECTED POEMS

EUNICE DE SOUZA

PENGUIN BOOKS

An imprint of Penguin Random House

PENGUIN BOOKS

USA | Canada | UK | Ireland | Australia
New Zealand | India | South Africa | China | Singapore

Penguin Books is an imprint of the Penguin Random House group of companies
whose addresses can be found at global.penguinrandomhouse.com

Published by Penguin Random House India Pvt. Ltd
4th Floor, Capital Tower 1, MG Road,
Gurugram 122 002, Haryana, India

Penguin
Random House
India

First published by Penguin Books India 2009
This extended edition published in Penguin Books by Penguin Random House
India 2025

Copyright © Melanie Silgardo 2025
Introduction © Vidyan Ravinthiran 2025

Fix first published by Newground, Mumbai, 1979
Women in Dutch Painting first published by Praxis, Mumbai, 1988
Ways of Belonging: Selected Poems first published by Polygon, Edinburgh, 1990
Selected and New Poems first published by St. Xavier's College, Mumbai, 1994
Dangerlok first published by Penguin Books India, New Delhi, 2001
A Necklace of Skulls first published by Penguin Books India, New Delhi, 2009
Learn from the Almond Leaf first published by Poetrywala,
Paperwall Publishing, 2016

All rights reserved

10 9 8 7 6 5 4 3 2

Please note that no part of this book may be used or reproduced in any manner
for the purpose of training artificial intelligence technologies or systems.

ISBN 9780143475217

Typeset in Bembo Std by Manipal Technologies Limited, Manipal

Printed at Repro India Limited

This book is sold subject to the condition that it shall not, by way of trade
or otherwise, be lent, resold, hired out or otherwise circulated without the
publisher's prior consent in any form of binding or cover other than that in
which it is published and without a similar condition including this condition
being imposed on the subsequent purchaser.

www.penguin.co.in

MIX
Paper from
responsible sources
FSC® C004727

This is a legitimate digitally printed version of the book and therefore might not
have certain extra finishing on the cover.

Eunice de Souza, 1998

Photograph by Madhu Kapparath

Contents

Early Poems (1969–89)

Women in Dutch Painting (1988)

Learn from the Almond Leaf (2016)

New Poems (2015–17)

Introduction

This book contains all Eunice de Souza's published poems, and also—at the end—works previously uncollected. Since I've written another essay about her that is available online ('Speech Acts', in the *Yale Review*), this introduction focuses on other poems—especially those of *Learn from the Almond Leaf*, published shortly before her death in 2017.

Varying the lively vernacular of the Bombay poets she knew and worked with (Arun Kolatkar designed the cover of her debut), de Souza extends 'a line of wit in Indian poetry in English by women' evinced by peers and followers she analysed and anthologized (I quote one of her sentences about Mamta Kalia), but with, too, a longer history: 'women have been writing poetry in India since about 1000 BCE on religious and secular themes.' 'When you write about yourself,' she says, 'you are also evoking others who have known similar experiences of claustrophobia, alienation, devaluation'; yet—splicing together her critical insights—'it is not useful, finally, to read back from the poetry into the life, in the case of Kamala Das or any other 'confessional' poet.' Reading 'My Students', my own students said they didn't know anyone wrote like this until extremely recently (they were thinking of twenty-first century, US, internetified poetry).

'A string of multicultural place names does not automatically create a resonant poem. Poems of this kind, in fact, often rely on an identity buzz or political correctness to do their work for them.' We too, are de Souza's students. Let's not disappoint her.

* * *

Eunice de Souza was born in 1940 in Pune to Goan Catholics. Modern lyric poems are sometimes attacked by both experimentalists and reactionaries for being, supposedly, mere anecdotes. But when de Souza writes in her first book, *Fix*—published in 1979—about Goa (deeply and idiosyncratically Portuguese, and still at that time a union territory), she doesn't repeat but frames (critiques, palpates both diagnostically and cherishingly) the structure of anecdote. Of nostalgic—the poem's called 'Idyll'—talk about the good old days:

> When Goa was Goa
> my grandfather says
> the bandits came
> over the mountain
> to our village
> only to splash
> in cool springs
> and visit Our Lady's Chapel.

The bandits prefigure modern tourists to Goa, which has over a hundred kilometres of coastline. The poem seems simple. Its lineation looks elementary, its syntax unadorned. You have to look, and hear, more closely.

Beginning with the title. Though we use the word loosely, an 'idyll' was, originally—returning to Theocritus—not a pastoral haven but a poem about such a place: a literary genre. An artificial creation, then—like the grandfather's word-picture of a paradise lost. The first line is tautologous. With the second, we realize this is, as labelled in fiction, free indirect style—emulating the grandfather's talk, preserving the contour of his opinionating voice. He means that Goa is not Goa any longer. Now blemished, it could, previously, resist spoliation: 'the bandits came' sounds ominous, as if this were about things ruined when *they* turned up, but the following lines amend this impression. Violence turns to play and relaxation ('splash'!) and the bandits may even convert, or have been converted already, to Catholicism—originating itself with incursion and conquest, under Portuguese control in the sixteenth century.

If, then, the poem scrutinizes a form of compensatory mythmaking, where it is said that violent outsiders are deflected, even transformed, by religion, it's also about how histories are constructed. Introducing *The Satthiandan Family Album*, de Souza remarks of Indian Christians that 'conversion certainly continues to be a contentious issue

[…] I, for one, have no interest in conversions, though my family is a product of conversions which took place in Goa a long time ago. Nevertheless, it interests me to know how people found the courage to leave family and friends to follow an idea in which they had come to believe'. To enquire into history, Goan and otherwise, is to consider the mutations of culture, as things imported and enforced are naturalized. This applies not only to religion but also the English language, which, though it was introduced to India by another colonizing power, de Souza considers her language—embracing it with gusto.

I've quoted roughly half of the poem. Here is the rest:

Old ladies were safe
among their bags
of rice and chillies,
unperturbed
when souls restless in purgatory
stoned roofs
to ask for prayers.
Even the snakes bit
only to break the monotony.

Isolating 'unperturbed' on its own line (it also resonates with 'purgatory'), de Souza breaks with the grandfather's style, now, of speech. Another voice arises: ironical, impatient with his rose-tinting of the past (which is also a resistance to the present, a mode of disapproval).

Other poems in *Fix* are transparently critical of Catholic patriarchy. In this case, de Souza's critique of the fantasy, of an age where women were safe from aggression (ascribed to restless souls, not living men) is harder to spot. It's an example, and I'll come back to this, of how we must read her poems with her other poems in mind, including those written decades ago. Unlike the grandfather, she doesn't draw a clean line between the present and the past but observes how painful events are retrospectively softened: apparently, the stones thrown at roofs are but a request, and—absurdly; it provides the poem with a joke-ending—the snakes only bite because they are bored, or since the people are.

We usually consider sound effects in poems in terms of mimesis. Generations of English schoolchildren have written that when Wilfred Owen describes in his 'Anthem For Doomed Youth' the 'stuttering rifles' rapid rattle', the jangling sounds emulate gunfire. Comparing in de Souza's poem the focusing of sound, as 'snakes bit' is succeeded by 'break', to the reverberance of 'unperturbed' and 'purgatory', we might instead see (hear) her sounds as generative of satiric emphasis. At these junctures, the poem, arising of the Goan culture it describes, considers its terms of relation as well as reference. I think of Arun

Kolatkar's verse about the temple-town of Jejuri, misread as straightforwardly Westernized and patronizing; also of Nissim Ezekiel's famous poem about a village mother who is bitten by a scorpion and concludes—following both religious and 'rationalist' attempts at treatment—'Thank God the scorpion picked on me / And spared my children'. These Indian poems inaugurate new styles, but it isn't a break with the past; more, of reconstruing inheritances toward the new. Culture, Kolatkar, Ezekiel and de Souza suggest, is what you do with what was done to you. Freedom is somewhere in the mix, glimpse-tasted in the instant before its disappearance.

* * *

De Souza taught for forty years in Mumbai, a city flooding and overheating at an extraordinary rate. Several poems from *Learn From The Almond Leaf* touch on the climate crisis. Poetry, notably elegy, found, once, reassurance in the recurrence of the seasons. 'O Wind', writes Percy Bysshe Shelley (he's also talking about political revolution), 'If Winter comes, can Spring be far behind?' An assumption both geographically and temporally specific: this far into the Anthropocene, seasons are exacerbated, or lose their original character. 'Western Ghats', de Souza's self-elegy, mocks the elegy-trope where nature goes into mourning: 'Fling my ashes in the Western Ghats / […] May the leopards develop / A taste for poetry. / […] May there be mist and waterfalls / Grass and flowers / in the wrong season'. And 'Close on the Heels' is more unreservedly an eco-poem:

> Close on the heels
> of a hot October
> comes a hot November
> a hot December.
> Somebody up there, down there,
> anywhere
> have mercy.

It is, almost, a prayer to 'somebody up there'. De Souza operates on the borderline between spirituality (not organized religion; besides Catholicism, she's critical of such Hinduistic ego-transcendence, as she considers a form of male privilege)—and scepticism. Her poems are dotted with moments of stillness one doesn't know whether or not to take at face value (in the following lines, from 'Travelling', is the rhyme validating or too cosy?): 'Wedged between houses, a sliver of sea, / casuarinas, clean sand, / infinity.' But 'Close on the Heels' is also a protest poem, aimed at those doing damage 'down' here.

'Summer', preceding it, mentions air polluted by Holi bonfires, and the title poem, first in the book, links fire as a trope of cosmic flux with the geopolitical devastation of a country going up in smoke:

> Learn from the almond leaf
> which flames as it falls.
> The ground is burning.
> The earth is burning.
> Flamboyance
> is all.

Minimalism meets symbolism. Turning to 'Remains', an even shorter poem:

> My mother's bones in a niche.
> My aunt's ashes likewise.
>
> A lifetime.
> A lifetime.

The repetition is a lament—wondering, disillusioned. (Compare 'My Mother Feared Death': 'Handed back to us in a plastic bag / her bones are forced into a niche. / 'I'm lonely,' she says. / I dream of her. / It's the best I can do.') But 'Remains' is also a concrete poem where 'a lifetime'—those two words, printed twice—set atop 'a lifetime' represents, spatially, the bones and ashes arranged together. Lives reduced to juxtaposed matter.

Returning to 'Summer'—there's a repetition here too, or almost. 'The ground is burning': it's covered by vibrant almond leaves. When the phrase deepens, to 'the earth is burning' ('earth', 'learn', and 'burning' sonically inflect the line), the environmental interpretation activates. Without taking over, since—coming up next—'Flamboyance / is all' alludes to Shakespeare: 'readiness is all' from *Hamlet*, and 'ripeness is all' from *King Lear*. It's one of those poems, like Elizabeth Bishop's 'One Art', where the person giving advice is also trying to persuade herself. *Women in Dutch Painting*, published in 1988, includes a string of poems either in this register or resisting it (when someone else buttonholes the poet): 'Advice to Women', 'From You I Have Understood', 'Songs of Survival' and 'Songs of Innocence', 'Transcend Self, You Say'. (There's also the early, previously unpublished, poem, 'At Veena's Wedding': 'There are no happy rebels, you said. / Settle down. Don't cut your nose / to spite your face.') People keen to advise others are, often, unsure of themselves; could it also be that the most stirring, enrapturing advice gains its power to convince from that very undecidedness?

Those who can, do. Those who can't, teach. Which isn't necessarily a slight on teachers—like de Souza, who taught for forty years at St. Xavier's College in Mumbai—but an insight into the counterintuitive intertwining in our psychologies, of transferrable conviction with feelings of precarity. Struggling to work things out ourselves, we gain the power to change the minds of others. 'Otherness/Wise' was published in 1994:

> I have spoken much of
> otherness
> and must now, alas,
> practise what I teach.

The expected idiom would be, 'practise what I preach', but de Souza chooses to reference her own profession. (Many boast of being poet-critics or poet-scholars but perhaps it is more meaningful to be a poet-teacher.) Although she was, to her students, a figure of considerable charismatic authority—her death brought forth many tributes—she was also extremely susceptible to the true or false suasions of others. Their suggestions, slights, encouragements and discouragements:

> At a conference in Delhi, the Australian poet A.D. Hope asked me to send him whatever I had written (I hadn't published a book yet) and wrote me a morale-boosting letter about the poems. I needed that boost because at the same conference, a Canadian academic told me that my poems weren't really poems because they didn't have images. This worried me because I was already unsure

of the rather jagged pieces I had produced when all I
wanted to write were lyrical poems with soft, sensuous
and passionate lines! Regardless of what I told my students,
only lyrical poetry seemed like 'real' poetry to me.

This relays the insecurities of an Indian writing in English—a
postcolonial poet in the Global South, outside networks of
literary esteem; it is also about, as a woman, being told
by men (I realize I'm making an assumption about that
'Canadian academic') that you either are or are not the
real deal. ('Soft, sensuous and passionate' are adjectives de
Souza applies to idealized poetry, but they also conjure
an idealized woman. She and her poems, intransigently
'jagged', cut like glass.)

Returning to my theme, we see her convincing her
students of the worth of a sort of poetry in which—at least
when *she's* writing it—she doesn't wholly believe. There's
no hypocrisy here. We all have doubts, and it is brave
to discuss them openly (which is not the same thing as,
self-indulgently). And a poem is a place where conviction
and doubt can live together, neither cancelling the other
out. So when de Souza says to burn brightly in the face
of death, I don't think we're meant either to read this as
an Instagrammable affirmation, or as a voice obscuring
with a show of boldness its own uncertainties. We are,
instead, to occupy both positions at once. To see moments

of declaration as occurring within a relational process susceptible to misgivings. She also notices in 'Reluctant Spring' that 'the last red leaf on the almond tree / refuses to fall'. Reluctance, coded as fear, blurs into refusal, a more heroic rebellion against the passing of time.

One way in which de Souza incorporates both thoughts and second thoughts, the interdependent troughs and peaks of feeling comprising a psychological terrain, is by writing, in her last book, sequels to poems from a long while back. 'Aubade 2', for instance, which (linking to the original 'Aubade', which I'll discuss in a moment, but also 'Idyll', which I already have) unsettles the expectation its title arouses: an aubade is a poem-song about lovers parting at dawn. De Souza's first 'Aubade', in her 1990 Selected, *Ways of Belonging*, subtly ghosts this separation: 'A line, a word, colour, rhythm / plangent in the mind's groove: / One sets them free— / to learn, finally learn / to claim nothing'. But it tallies, too, with her poems about teaching, since a teacher must, finally, set her students free 'to learn' under their own steam. And there's a slight, extra tension to that dash-enhanced line-break, because really, it's the poet herself with something to learn.

'Aubade 2' is also about letting go of refusing to let go:

We talk across continents.
It's unlikely we'll meet again.

Can't smoke, can't travel,
and certainly no heaven.
A cold wind at our backs
we abjure philosophy.
Done with errant lovers, husbands,
not quite wise old birds.
We're still the age at which we met.

I have read and re-read this poem, trying to figure out
its secret—why it affects me so. The smoke resonates
with the collection's imagery of fire. And the last line is
vital. It compresses two meanings into one: it's when the
two women speak on the phone, that they feel they are
again 'the age at which we met'; there's also the sense
that none of us really ever change, that time passes like
a dream.

'The Road', from *Women in Dutch Painting*, begins with
de Souza as a child emerging from church, being gossiped
at and about in school. It ends in another here and now that
overlays and resurrects a there and then. Another kind of
'still' moment:

I clutched Sister Flora's skirt
and cried for my mother
who taught across the road.
Sister Flora is dead.

The school is still standing.
I am still learning to cross the road.

Learning, again, and failing to learn. What does it mean—returning to 'Aubade 2'—to 'abjure philosophy'? Shakespeare's Prospero discards his sorcery before returning to public governance: 'this rough magic / I here abjure'. These 'wise old birds' aren't going anywhere, they are moving out of life, not into it. Under no illusions about what comes next: 'certainly no heaven'.

* * *

Why are the poems of Eunice de Souza essential to me? For their tight technique, the speech-rhythms in them that never cloy—certainly; but mostly, I think, for the push-and-pull they evince, outlining piecemeal (with evasions and misdirection, then direct, precipitous glimpses) a personality pursuing an impracticable equilibrium. She won't disavow even the most unpleasant experiences and emotions, since they're part of what it means to be alive. In 'Songs of Survival', the poet tells herself:

Don't flail.
Don't let the hurt show.
Not even this afternoon
can last forever.

De Souza is a formidable analyst of our ever-altering (but sometimes horrifically permanent-seeming) emotional states—those 'moods of one's mind' which Keats, in his verse-letter to his friend Reynolds, tries to push away. *This too will pass*, de Souza tells herself. Maintain your dignity, 'don't flail.' Yet in 'Remember Medusa?', she—the voice finding and exploring various postures—discards stoicism:

> Better the flailing
> the angry words
> burning through the brain
> the certain sorrow
>
> than letting go than the fall
> slow-motion
> into the abyss

Anger can be terrible when it so thoroughly colonizes you as to exclude every nuance of thought and feeling; it can be awful to be seen to be angry, for it to become public knowledge that you were strongly affected by someone or something, to the point of losing control. We go over such memories and cringe. But both fury and embarrassment are expressions of what it means to be alive. De Souza wishes, often, to plunge into the destructive element. At other times, she would get away from it all—this is where the spirituality I've mentioned comes in—finding in female friendship a space and a place of, more than safety, personal and political nourishment.

'Invitation', first published in her previous Collected, *A Necklace of Skulls*, invites us to think about private and public life and how they either come together or remain separated by walls of privilege and delusion. Virginia Woolf said women needed a room of their own (and a private income) to write. For de Souza, any zone into which one could retreat from the world is at best temporary—hardly vacuum-sealed. But our yearnings for such a place are to be seriously considered, as part and parcel of modernity. They correspond to our interpellation into a public sphere where genuine conflicts (to do with, for example, in de Souza's earlier poems, religious sexism, or, later, the destruction of the planet), also have a way of turning unreal, into sound and fury signifying nothing.

She tempts me with a vision of hills
grass that's green
peacocks as common as sparrows

We can read in the courtyard, she says,
to the sound of the woodpecker working his tree,
admire her roses, pluck fruit, count stars.
Bring aunt, dogs, parakeet, she says,
write a happy poem or two.
Once in a way, she says,

> we'll take a little walk to the village
> to find out how the world's
> not getting on.

De Souza remains tied to that world of people 'not getting on'. She wasn't only a poet, critic and novelist: she also wrote an opinion-column for the *Mumbai Mirror*. She was more than aware of how information blurs into misinformation and news into fake news—in both the local (she writes brilliantly about gossip) and global 'village'.

'She tempts me', the poem begins, liminally invoking the (misogynistic) idea of the woman as temptress, before shifting—'with a vision'—to reference Jesus tempted by Satan in the wilderness. As with the Prospero allusion in 'Aubade 2', de Souza flips things around. The temptation lies not in spaces of urban power but in the desire to escape them, to what resembles a writers' retreat. Where it's suggested she'll write happy, not unhappy poems, inspired by her new, nature-adjacent surroundings; where the only male presences, notably, are peacocks and the woodpecker (de Souza's poems about pets are often also about male-female relations).

By allowing its vision of paradise—resembling the grandfather's fantasy in 'Idyll', but in fact deeply different—to expand and become, in and through language, materially present, 'Invitation' quietly indicts an overloud public sphere. 'Not getting on' is both a funny and serious, a bathetic and capacious variation on the idiom we expect. To 'get on in the world' is to prosper materially, often at the expense of others; to say people have failed to 'get on' is to suggest they've fallen out over inconsequential matters rather than genuine differences or inequalities. So de Souza's surprising end to her poem includes both real and unreal disagreements over both real and unreal issues; more than that, it suggests that it's never easy, and sometimes impossible, to disintricate these things. In a way that isn't at all escapist, she suggests the necessity for women, in particular, of spaces outside the frenzied agora, where—as not a denial, but a condition, of citizenship—life can be lived and thought about seriously.

A second idiom is played with earlier. 'Once in a way' leaps out at me, being (like 'did you enjoy?', the locution analysed in another poem, 'Return') shared with my Sri Lankan Tamil family. 'Once in a way', my mother says, not 'once in a while'. Reassurance mixes with resignation, encouragement blurs into compromise, in a manner unique to this South Asian English sentence-sound. De Souza repeats the speech tag 'she says' three times, and when 'says' and 'way' make each other prominent in this line, it is at this moment that the person extending the invitation to the speaker is both sensitively characterized—through her style of speech—and, where a distance opens up between her, and the poet who recognizes that no total separation from the public world is possible. 'She says': so *she says*, is another idiom coming to mind; the invitation is too good to be true. Since there exists in both women a relational pull drawing them once again, with a curiosity that wishes to remain aloof but is, in fact, passional, back to 'the world' that's 'not getting on'. ('The heart is stilled', writes de Souza, in 'The Hills Heal', 'by the blue flash / of a lone jay's wing [...] // Yet the world will maul again, I know, / and I'll go gladly for the usual price'.) I think, though it's anachronistic, of those addicted to social media; also of how one of the disguises this addiction takes is that of political engagement.

As creatures venting more or less uncontrollably gouts of both spite and fellow-feeling, we tell ourselves that the expression of these impulses links in a clear-cut way to action changing the world for the better, even though this isn't necessarily the case. 'Once in a way'—that slightly awry phrase—suggests the women can contain an impulse, domesticate it. But is this true? 'Invitation' manifests and reveals a series of interlocking and perhaps inescapable emotional manoeuvres. Even if de Souza's poetry weren't so intensely relevant to today's politics and poetics, it would be worth reading. But that relevance seems to me so strong as to astonish: I wonder if this new edition will leave you feeling the same way.

Vidyan Ravinthiran
January 2025

Fix (1979)

Catholic Mother

Francis X. D'Souza
father of the year.
Here he is top left
the one smiling.
By the Grace of God he says
we've had seven children
(in seven years)
We're One Big Happy Family
God Always Provides
India will Suffer for
her Wicked Ways
(these Hindu buggers got no ethics)
Pillar of the Church
says the parish priest
Lovely Catholic Family
says Mother Superior
the pillar's wife
says nothing.

Marriages Are Made

My cousin Elena
is to be married.
The formalities
have been completed:
her family history examined
for TB and madness
her father declared solvent
her eyes examined for squints
her teeth for cavities
her stools for the possible
non-Brahmin worm.
She's not quite tall enough
and not quite full enough
(children will take care of that)
Her complexion it was decided
would compensate, being just about
the right shade
of rightness
to do justice to
Francisco X. Noronha Prabhu
good son of Mother Church.

Feeding the Poor at Christmas

Every Christmas we feed the poor.
We arrive an hour late: Poor dears,
like children waiting for a treat.
Bring your plates. Don't move.
Don't try turning up for more.
No. Even if you don't drink
you can't take your share
for your husband. Say thank you
and a rosary for us every evening.
No. Not a towel *and* a shirt,
even if they're old.
What's that you said?
You're a good man, Robert, yes,
beggars can't be, exactly.

Sweet Sixteen

Well, you can't say
they didn't try.
Mamas never mentioned menses.
A nun screamed: You vulgar girl
don't say brassières
say bracelets.
She pinned paper sleeves
onto our sleeveless dresses.
The preacher thundered:
Never go with a man alone
Never alone
and even if you're engaged
only passionless kisses.
At sixteen, Phoebe asked me:
Can it happen when you're in a dance hall
I mean, you know what,
getting *preggers* and all that, *when*
you're dancing?
I, sixteen, assured her
you could.

Miss Louise

She dreamt of descending
curving staircases
ivory fan aflutter
of children in sailor suits
and organza dresses
till the dream rotted her innards
but no one knew:
innards weren't permitted
in her time.
Shaking her greying ringlets:
'My girl, I can't even
go to Church you know
I unsettle the priests
so completely. Only yesterday
that handsome Fr Hans was saying,
"Miss Louise, I feel an arrow
through my heart."
But no one will believe me
if I tell them. It's always
been the same. They'll say,
"Yes Louisa, we know, professors
loved you in your youth,
judges in your prime."'

Mrs Hermione Gonsalvez

Mrs Hermione Gonsalvez says:
In the good old days
I had looks *and* colour
now I've got only colour
just look at my parents
how they married me to a dark man
on my own I wouldn't even have
looked at him. Once we were going
somewhere for a holiday and I went on
ahead my hubby was to come later
and there were lots of fair
Maharashtrian ladies there and they
all said Mrs Gonsalvez how fair and
beautiful you are your husband must be
so good-looking too but when Gonsalvez came
they all screamed
and ran inside their houses
thinking the devil had come.

Bandra Christian Party

Hubby emerges from coal bin
bottles under arm
face a smirk.
Hot stuff, he says.
The gathered goans giggle.
Dirty jokes:
hot stuff and sex.
Fred the comic slaps hubby
on back
now the party'll go men go
says Fred
goans agaggle
Fred laughing loudest
(he's the big thing
this side of Hill Rd)
What personality says Dominic
such pink lips men and
look at that chest
so comic says Mabel
keeps the crowd going
says Hetty
Fred is the life of the party.
Come on men Fred give us

a song calls Mabel
What personality says Dominic
such pink lips and look
at that chest.

St Anthony's Shrine

The beggars line up early
cry unrelentingly for alms.
The faithful come bringing
flowers, candles, money,
and pray for lost handbags,
lost souls, lost jobs.
Last week there was a miracle.
Alleluia D'Souza
Founder of the Shrine
emerges at ten.
'Alleluia, Mary Gomes'
mother is dying.
Alleluia, my son
found a house.
Alleluia, pray for me
to St Anthony.
Alleluia, my wife's returned.'
Alleluia stands by the shrine door
with bread she has
baked and broken.
'Take my child,'
she says to each,
'This is the bread

St Anthony has given.'
'May the bread turn to
scorpions,' says the parish
priest. 'The people miss Mass
but not St Anthony's.'
The bishop says, 'Alleluia
is a good soul. She donated
a Frigidaire last year to the
orphanage.'

Anniversary

Today, in his honour,
Mrs Lobo will not quarrel
with Mrs Lopez
about who should decorate
the altar and how.
The Men's Sodality will bring him
a box of cigars as they've done
for twenty years.
The girls of the parish will sing
May Your Path Be Strewn With Roses.
He sees it still:
I shall be a colt
mother when I grow up
a colt untamed
striking fire off rocks
his mother weeps
not knowing why.

Varca, 1942

The Archbishop said:
Great landlords and peasants
must worship together
The peasants cannot walk to a church
an hour away
So the great landlords of Varca
shot at their Archbishop
and the Archbishop
barred the Church doors and said
No landlord will enter the Church
in Varca or any other Church
in Christendom again
Devils will not be cast out
of the newborn
the dying will not be blessed
with holy oils
After many months
the Archbishop relented
and the landlords repented
and everyone worshipped together
And the landlords were landlords
and the peasants peasants
ever after.

Conversation Piece

My Portuguese-bred colleague
picked up a clay shivalingam
one day and said:
Is this an ashtray?
No, said the salesman,
This is our god.

Idyll

When Goa was Goa
my grandfather says
the bandits came
over the mountain
to our village
only to splash
in cool springs
and visit Our Lady's Chapel.
Old ladies were safe
among their bags
of rice and chillies,
unperturbed
when souls restless in purgatory
stoned roofs
to ask for prayers.
Even the snakes bit
only to break the monotony.

Omen

Today
that utterly respectable
big brown clock
in the college staff room
decided to move its hands
backwards.
No one is surprised.

My Students

My students think it funny
that Daruwallas and de Souzas
should write poetry.
Poetry is faery lands forlorn.
Women writers Miss Austen.
Only foreign men air their crotches.

Poem for a Poet

It pays to be a poet.
You don't have to pay prostitutes.
Marie has spiritual thingummies.
Write her a poem about the
Holy Ghost. Say:
'Marie, my frequent sexual encounters
represent more than an attempt
to find mere physical fulfilment.
They are a poet's struggle to
transcend the self
and enter into
communion
with the world.'
Marie's eyes will glow.
Pentecostal flames will descend.
The Holy Ghost will tremble inside her.
She will babble in strange tongues:
'O Universal Lover
in a state of perpetual erection!
Let me too enter into
communion with the world
through thee.'
Ritu loves music and

has made a hobby of psychology.
Undergraduate, and better still,
uninitiated.
Write her a poem about woman flesh.
Watch her become oh so womanly and grateful.
Giggle with her about
horrid mother keeping an eye
on the pair, the would-be babes
in the wood, and everything will be
so idyllic, so romantic
so *intime*
Except, that you, big deal,
are forty-six
and know what works
with whom.

He Speaks

Well, now tell me
what would you do to a
woman who wrote to you
saying: You haven't written
for three weeks. You're the
meanest man alive. Not even
an exclamation mark at the end
and she sends telegrams and
express letters saying it was
a joke, love, it was a joke.
I did what any self-respecting
man would. I ignored her for
a week. Her pleadings wore
me down. She was an affectionate
creature and tried hard, poor dear,
but never quite made the grade.
She *would* walk too close to me
and then protest naively: How
should lovers walk? Show me.
Ridiculous, too, her unseemly
mirth when I said confidentially
I have such an hypnotic effect
on women. Everywhere I go

they fall into my arms.
Jamie Bond! she cried
My man is India's answer to
Jamie Bond!
After that pathological display
I decided there was only one
thing to do: fix her.
The next time we were making love
I said quite casually:
I hope you realize I do this
with other women.

For a Child, Not Clever

Once you thought it good
you came fifty-sixth in class
out of fifty-six children.
But Mummy, you said,
fifty-six is bigger than one.
Voices crackle and break
around you. Why do you provoke
your sisters? Why do you never
tell us about your tests?
To me, the cousin who visits
sometimes, you say, as if
explaining things: I'm not clever,
you see, that's why these things
keep happening.
You have pierced me with your pain
dunce dunce double 'd'
Suddenly I see
how it's possible in Gethsamene
to say: I am the one you seek.
Let the rest go free.

My Grandfather's Death

They didn't nail down the lid
of the coffin, in front of us.
Nobody insisted I throw gravel.
They left him a little while
in the quiet February sun.
They were kind.
They didn't frighten anyone
make anyone feel how they'd
suffocate there
though they were dead.
Thirty years ago they
buried my father there.
That was a different kind of
death. They didn't know
I often asked
'What have they done to my daddy?'
and that nobody could explain.

Forgive Me, Mother

Forgive me, mother,
that I left you
a life-long widow
old, alone.
It was kill or die
and you got me anyway:
The blood congeals at lover's touch
The guts dissolve in shit.
I was never young.
Now I'm old, alone.
In dreams
I hack you.

For My Father, Dead Young

I hold the child up in delight.
The revolving fan cuts her through.
It's a dream.
I'm you.
I heard your fumblings in the dark.
Woke on wet beds.
Kniving marshes
I'm you.
You're the cold wind.
The grey mist.
The black dawn. The grinning skull.
I'm you.

de Souza Prabhu

No, I'm not going to
delve deep down and discover
I'm really de Souza Prabhu
even if Prabhu was no fool
and got the best of both worlds.
(Catholic Brahmin!
I can hear his fat chuckle still)
No matter that
my name is Greek
my surname Portuguese
my language alien.
There are ways
of belonging.
I belong with the lame ducks.
I heard it said
my parents wanted a boy.
I've done my best to qualify.
I hid the bloodstains
on my clothes
and let my breasts sag.
Words the weapon
to crucify.

This Swine of Gadarene*

This swine of Gadarene
has stopped his hurtle
to the sea.
No. The demons
haven't lost interest in him.
He feels
posthumous.
Behind him
the dead land.
Ahead
the dead sea.
For a little while yet, he says,
let me chew stubble.

---

* A district south-east of Galilee. Christ cured two men possessed by evil
spirits here and compelled the devils to enter a herd of swine which then
threw themselves off a cliff and were drowned.

Autobiographical

Right, now here it comes.
I killed my father when I was three.
I have muddled through several affairs
and always come out badly.
I've learned almost nothing from experience.
I head for the abyss with
monotonous regularity.
My enemies say I'm a critic because
really I'm writhing with envy
and anyway need to get married.
My friends say I'm not
entirely without talent.
Yes, I've tried suicide,
I tidied my clothes but
left no notes. I was surprised
to wake up in the morning.
One day my soul
stood outside me
watching me twitch
and grin and gibber
the skin tight
over my bones
I thought the whole world

was trying to rip me up
cut me down go through me
with a razor blade
then I discovered
a cliché: that's what I wanted
to do to the world.

One Man's Poetry

Irony as an attitude to life
is passé, you said.
So be it, friend.
Let me be passé and survive.
Leave me the cutting edge of words
to clear a world
for my ego.
The rage is almost done.
My soul's almost my own.
Chances are
my father himself
didn't wish to die.
My mother watched by his bedside
and never forgave herself
for being asleep
the night he died.
He left a desk, a chair,
a typewriter and a notebook.
At family gatherings
my mother smiled
in her best faded chiffon
and travelled third
with her in-laws travelling first

in the same train.
As I grew up
I longed only
to laugh easily.
All that emerged
was a nervous whinny.
My limbs began to scatter
my face dissolve
my love would hold me close
for hours when I could
neither speak nor weep,
bring me food and feed me.
From him I am learning to love.

Early Poems (1969–89)

At Veena's Wedding

There are no happy rebels, you said.
Settle down. Don't cut your nose
to spite your face.
Watching you touch your father's feet
the glow of gold in your hair
I too feel joy
in the unbroken gesture
I too was dandled
on a father's knee
watched worlds
revolve around me.

Star-Gazing

The light I saw in you
love
came from a dead star.
I am to blame for this:
star-gazing at my age
is an ambiguous art.

I Want a Father

I want a father;
always have.
God won't do.
He's too judgemental.
And so I found you—
Like my father, absent.

Fledgling

I am grateful
the sparrows have made
my house their home.
All those months they stayed away
I waited for their return.
Soon the fledgling will cling
wide-eyed, to the pelmet
as generations of wide-eyed fledglings
have done.
The mother scolds and chatters
forgetting
shadows which circle the sun.

Rowanlake

Only the skin under your eyes
tells me you are older.
We could have been happy, you say
in India or Brazil. You still want
to wring your mother's neck.
You want to know if you
ruined my name.
It's your little daughter now
who tries hard to make me feel
ill at ease.
I can be polite to mother and daughter—
in twenty years one learns
all sorts of things.
Your pleasure in this meeting
comes when at long last
I am alone but unafraid.

'It's too late for me'

It's too late for me
to die young
as you did.
You left no words
to teach me
the secret of your courage.
I cling to little things—
a glossy new leaf
a singing bird at dawn
I close my eyes
on the long train rides
through this crumbling city
I convince myself
this method's painful
that one messy
that living does not desecrate
your memory.

Grandmother

My grandmother was fourteen
when she married.
We've lost that photograph of her
with gold combs in her hair.
She was beautiful
bore seven children
and often ran home
to her mother.
She and the servants
spoke the same language
of silence.

Family Gossip

St Christiana lived long before
ODORONO made the scene and
St Christiana hated
the smell of people.
It made her nostrils quiver
just to see them coming
and even their best friends
didn't tell them
to stop crowding her.
So what could she do poor thing
but take right off
and hover near the ceiling
in a rage.
But bless me if they didn't
just stand there
gawping.

'He's married, has a child'

He's married, has a child,
another on the way—
is proud his family has been here
for generations
before the hills were quarried
and trees torn up by those
who could not count the years
it takes a tree to grow.
He finds my style a trifle hard, but
understated, urbane, witty.
I understand the call of child, and tree
and mountain spring:
He hasn't learned their language yet,
will freeze if I say
I need you, hold me.
His strength, cast-iron fidelity.

Women in Dutch Painting
(1988)

Women in Dutch Painting

(for Melanie Silgardo)

The afternoon sun is on their faces.
They are calm, not stupid,
pregnant, not bovine.
I know women like that
and not just in paintings—
an aunt who did not answer her husband back
not because she was plain
and Anna who writes poems
and hopes her avocado stones
will sprout in the kitchen.
Her voice is oatmeal and honey.

Pilgrim

The hills crawl with convoys.
Slow lights wind round
and down the dark ridges
to yet another
termite city.
The red god rock
watches all that passes.
He spoke once.
The blood-red boulders
are his witness.
God rock, I'm a pilgrim.
Tell me—
Where does the heart find rest?

Monsoon Journey

This time the mountains
were hidden by mist.
My lover is like smoke
my dearest friend far away
He writes with so much love
of the undiminished pleasure
of the text
the cadence and economy of poetry
of skies warm and generous
and of Simone Weil who says
grace fills empty spaces
where there is a void to receive it.
It is grace itself
which makes this void.
We are on the brink.

The Hills Heal

(for Veronik Jussawalla)

The hills heal as no hand does.
The heart is stilled by the blue flash
of a lone jay's wing.
Impossible to forget, you think,
the shadows of the sun here ever purple,
the receding plains where the wind still blows.
Yet the world will maul again, I know,
and I'll go gladly for the usual price,
emerge to flay myself in poems,
the sluiced vein just a formal close.

She and I

Perhaps he never died.
We've mourned him separately,
in silence,
she and I.
Suddenly, at seventy-eight,
she tells me his jokes,
his stories, the names of
paintings he loved,
and of some forgotten place
where blue flowers fell.
I am afraid
for her, for myself,
but can say nothing.

I Choose Not to Marry You, Love

I choose not to marry you, love.
There is poison in my tongue.
I maul. I calcify. I am a rib again.
I touch the world.
Stars turn black holes.

Eunice

Eunice, Embroidery Sister said
this petticoat you've cut
these seams
are worthy of an elephant
my dear
Silly bra-less bitch
Eunice is writing bad words sister
she's sewing up her head
for the third time sister
the limbs keep flopping
the sawdust keeps popping
out of the gaps
sister.

Remember Medusa?

My dumb ox loyalty is
the frozen heart
the frozen stare
of long aloneness
unpeopled even by terror
Remember Medusa,
who could not love
even herself?
Better the flailing
the angry words
burning through the brain
the certain sorrow
than letting go than the fall
slow-motion
into that abyss
Each life-line of words
years in the making.

Another Way to Die

Being eaten by maggots
is fantasy
The real thing is
to touch the outlines
of the hands, the hair
to find no body there
In a few hours
or a few days
the bits reassemble
a breast flies back
a dull pain
where the heart should be
an ache for a touch
or a quarrel
For a while again
you are almost
human.

For S. Who Wonders If I Get Much Joy
Out of Life

As a matter of fact I do.
I contemplate, with a certain
grim satisfaction
dynamic men who sell better butter.
Sometimes I down a Coke
implacably at the Taj.
This morning I terrorized
(successfully)
the bank manager.
I look striking in red and black
and a necklace of skulls.

Alibi

My love says
for god's sake
don't write poems
which heave and pant
and resound to the music
of our thighs
etc.
Just keep at what you are:
a sour old puss in verse
and leave the rest to me.

Advice to Women

Keep cats
if you want to learn to cope with
the otherness of lovers.
Otherness is not always neglect—
Cats return to their litter trays
when they need to.
Don't cuss out of the window
at their enemies.
That stare of perpetual surprise
in those great green eyes
will teach you
to die alone.

Reprieve

This poem is for you.
It's a reprieve.
It says
nothing in your little black heart
can frighten me,
I've looked too long
into my own.
Thank you for the gift
of your uncertainties.

The Road

(for Deepak Ananth)

As we came out of the church
into the sunlight
a row of small girls
in first communion dresses
I felt the occasion demanded
lofty thoughts.
I remember
only my grandmother
smiling at me.
They said
now she wears lipstick
now she is a Bombay girl
they said, your mother is lonely.
Nobody said, even the young must live.
In school
I clutched Sister Flora's skirt
and cried for my mother
who taught across the road.
Sister Flora is dead.
The school is still standing.
I am still learning
to cross the road.

From You I Have Understood

From you I have understood
something of the silence of gods
how they tire of being the first cause
of every quarrel
how they shrink
from sweaty importunity.
Even the skies these days
are full of junk in orbit.
Be less like the wild gods, love.

Unfinished Poem

I found your unfinished poem:
There's a sun in the sky
and you are near me
and all should be right with the world.
But something hasn't set
(and it had better not be the sun!)
I could pinch a line from Neruda for you:
'I want/to do with you what spring does/
with the cherry trees.'
There you have it: the apparent ease
of love and poetry.

October 30, 1987

For you I wrote
'I don't need words
any more.'
Now garrulous
with memories.

Songs of Survival

I
Don't write of self?
Self is a survivor-casualty
moan-mongering tragi-comedy
recalcitrant matter
mixed metaphor
struggling to breathe
in an odour of sanctity.
Trees are dusty
but condoms are blue.
Self detests platitudes.
Like you.

II
jackself
I can bludgeon you
no more
take pity
say forgive
Let me grow
as the grass grows
stanch
the primal wounding

jackself
say forgive

III
Nothing is ever still:
Rocks move. Rivers move.
Time passes.
Allow me my tailspin.
One day I'll find my axis
and revolve around the sun.

IV
Don't flail.
Don't let the hurt show.
Not even this afternoon
can last forever.
Perhaps you'll hear kindness
in a casual greeting.
Practice grave courtesy:
there are no tears in the
eye of the storm.
Survive to know you can.
There is little to be said
for suffering.

Songs of Innocence

I

Who made you?
God made me.
Why did he make you?
To know him, to love him
to be happy with him forever
in this world and the next.

II

orange berries in the backyard
goldfish in the pond
the sun high in the sky
uncles who make you feel tall
no myth in such memories
no chill in the dawn
marigold mood
before the fall

III

I crave your dream of innocence:
a profusion of flowers blooming
for themselves
birds big enough to swallow avocado stones

But green can be
humid as the womb . . .
Avoid, friend, the man who has never known
a dry season.

IV
Searching for roots
I find the caretaker dead
the white ants burrowing
grand-aunt clothed in cobwebs.
Her clock
crumbles in my hands.
Pink cement houses
surge up among the fronds.
I hear the pigs forage
and know this is not home.
This never was home:
grandfather left as a young man . . .
He had a well of sand.
To him more sand was given.

Transcend Self, You Say

Transcend self, you say.
Connect with myth, history,
the world crumbling around you.
Men can, and do. Beggars survive.
Destitutes survive. There's something in this culture.
Must ask beggars how they do it.
Smart arse. Poetess.
Friend, the histories I know aren't fit to print.
Remember Padma, widowed at seventeen,
Forbidden to see the sun for a year,
allowed out to crap only at night
when the pure were out of the way?
The perfect book is
one long cry in the dark.
A novelist said that,
who spent his life wondering why,
when the Nazis came,
his mother pushed *him* into a closet,
and let his sisters go to Auschwitz.

Meditation

The lonely ask too much and then
too little
chill the air with intensities
of longing or self-diminishment
cannot decide which is worse
the insularity of confidence
or the insularity of isolation
are hectored by those who've found
the motto in the cracker barrel
know kindness from those who
sometimes take risks.

Don't Look for My Life in These Poems

Poems can have order, sanity,
aesthetic distance from debris.
All I've learnt from pain
I always knew,
but could not do.

'And she lived happily ever after'

And she lived happily ever after.
Or perhaps reasonably happy
for some of the time.
Infancy and grand passions
are exhausting modes of seeing.
Now the grey sky is a sky
not a pall
the crocuses are allowed
their hesitations
friends and lovers
their friends and sometimes
even their lovers.
As the days grow longer she sees
students, friends, mother, aunts,
not always there,
but on call, often enough.

Visit

I like to visit you, you say.
You're always calm and smiling.
Should I tell you, I wonder,
I was a burly little girl
who knocked her sissy cousins down?
Unsure of your welcome
you entertain me with stories
of kleptomaniac uncles
and bootlegging aunts
the laughter suddenly dying
in your throat.
Have I seen, you wonder,
a shot dog drag its entrails home?

For Rita's Daughter, Just Born

Luminous new leaf
May the sun rise gently
on your unfurling
in the courtyard always linger
the smell of earth after rain
the stone of these steps
stay cool and old
gods in the niches
old brass on the wall
never the shrill cry of kites.

Home for the Aged, Sydney

They came into the world stone cold,
faces furrowed with dark rain.
Nobody called them.
They have no history.
More chilling than fiction
the lives of those
so marked for sorrow.
The sun rises and sets,
rises and sets.

Five London Pieces

I
Wintering in London

I can't feel the edge of my sari
and stumble
a stump in shoes.
My coat-sleeve knocks down
a glass of lager in a pub.
I ask for sherry at a party
where only white wine is served.
I long for the downs
which stay green in winter.

II
Encounter at a London Party

For a minute we stand blankly together.
You wonder in what language to speak to me,
offer a pickled onion on a stick instead.
You are young and perhaps forgetful
that the Empire lives
only in the pure vowel sounds I offer you
above the din.

III
Meeting Poets

Meeting poets I am disconcerted sometimes
by the colour of their socks
the suspicion of a wig
the wasp in the voice
and an air, sometimes, of dankness.
Best to meet in poems:
cool speckled shells
in which one hears
a sad but distant sea.

IV
A Good Day

It's been a good day.
My lover has been
unusually witty.
I have found a new
Baudelaire.
The poet next door has told me
some disgraceful stories.
My muse is tapping out a message
on my Olivetti:
at least today

write a poem with some
fizz in it.

V

In Wittersham
(for Ruth Fainlight)

Peace is a wide, flat, silent marsh
with fat sheep grazing on it.
They're a special breed here
resistant to water underfoot
and anyway the marsh
has almost been drained.
I chat with a neighbour
about December roses.
A visitor here,
I want nothing to change.
Yet many planes are still found
in the marshes,
identification tags intact,
and the town five miles away
was sacked and burned three times.

Return

I
The old wrought–iron gate has gone
with the tall tangled grass
and the mosquitoes.
The priest is chanting his blessings
on the stone of the new building.
Squirrels chase each other up and down
the two mango trees left standing.
My neighbours want to know,
did I enjoy?
Thinking of the old wrought–iron gate
and the cotton tree
that managed only one flower every summer
I agree, perhaps enjoyment
should have no object.

II
It was the sound of the shehnai
in a London flat
that brought me scurrying back
to catch this train
to be again among

these old hills
stray bougainvillea
and the peasant women
with only a handful of berries to sell.

III
I covet the presence your home has.
I want to be like that:
cool, dark, subterranean.
There I would not covet even you,
grudge your many loves
or even write you more love poems.

IV
Sarla Devi, Kusum Bala, Rani Devi,
all of ill fame.
I read your story in
the morning paper:
you refuse to wear ankle-bells
worn for generations
you study law
you hear catcalls in the street
drums and bells behind your books.
Sitting alone in a Bombay restaurant,
listening to the innuendoes of college clerks

and a loose-lipped Spanish priest,
I know something
of how you feel.

V
Tuka, forgive my familiarity.
I have loved your pithy verses
ever since that French priest
everyone thought mad
recited them, and told us
of his journey with your people.
They have broken down whole streets
of houses in Pandarpur, to widen
the road to the shrine.
The priests do not sound like you
but I'll offer a coconut anyway
for someone I love.
You made life hard for your wife
and I'm not sure I approve of that.
Nor did you heed her last request:
Come back soon.

From *Ways of Belonging: Selected Poems* (1990)

Notations

They needed so few notations
those unknown singers:
a dying queen, a faithless king,
a golden chain, the lover lost
in the dark forest of passion,
nobly lost, ignobly lost,
always they sang of loss.
No attempt to cauterize memory
no gestures of refusal
or acceptance. No cut to abstractions.
It happened: that is all they say.
It happened.

Aubade

So you are going too, my love,
the last, most beautiful
of my children:
a Botticelli, crystalline,
the pure ice-blue
of a southern ocean.
A line, a word, colour, rhythm
plangent in the mind's groove:
One sets them free—
to learn, finally learn
to claim nothing.

God Rock

There's a continent moving
under my feet, god rock.
In a million years
it will swallow the seas,
spew out mountains,
reduce this land
to a handful of gravel.
Give us a sign, god rock.
A city burns.

God Rock's Passion

God rock plunged into
the belly of the earth, molten.
Heaved off,
goat pellet seed.
Primeval slob.

Aravalli

The hills are splattered with
sacred linga, silicon-breast domes,
rivers sucked dry.
Predatory winds scorn paradox:
The hills are toads, fangs, skulls.
The chameleon, mottled grey like the rocks
barely breathes—
eyes half closed in meditation,
undivided in its aims.

Bequest

In every Catholic home there's a picture
of Christ holding his bleeding heart
in his hand.
I used to think, ugh.
The only person with whom
I have not exchanged confidences
is my hairdresser.
Some recommend stern standards,
others say float along.
He says, take it as it comes,
meaning, of course, as he hands it out.
I wish I could be a
Wise Woman
smiling endlessly, vacuously
like a plastic flower,
saying Child, learn from me.
It's time to perform an act of charity
to myself,
bequeath the heart, like a
spare kidney—
preferably to an enemy.

General Ward

'Imagine, she hasn't visited her mother
for three days!'
'What kind of daughter.'
Simple Christian sentiments,
simply kindly people who
plait the neglected mother's hair,
fetch her a glass of milk,
ring the bell for recalcitrant nurses.
How shall I say to them: in your simple words
I hear the subtle joy of
the guilt trip, the guilt whip?
Even the visitors in the ward,
confident in red and yellow taffeta dresses
feel their taffeta hearts go tsk tsk.
The Neglected Mother smiles at me
to pull me into the circle of sympathy.

Juhu Beach

So we visit my actor-friend in his home on the beach.
It's a squatter settlement, each home 5' by 3'.
He can hardly stand up in it. We can't breathe.
I stub out my cigarette on a sandbag.
Ramu, a neighbour, prepares the meal.
He used to be 'a joker' in the circus, but ran away,
couldn't take the threats, the beatings, the pay.
Through the gap that passes for a door
I watch the tide come in.
Once we had sat on a spot not far from here,
my actor-friend and I.
A stray dog adopted us and barked at passers-by.
It was my birthday. We feasted on pineapple cream pastries,
the dog, my friend and I.

From *Selected and New Poems* (1994)

Landscape

I

M. assures me she'll be back
to fling my ashes in the local creek
(We're short on sacred rivers here)
The pungent air will suit my soul.
It will find its place among
the plastic carrier bags and rags that float upstream
or is it downstream.
One can never tell.
The sea sends everything reeling back.
The trees go under.

II

We push so much under the carpet—
the carpet's now a landscape
A worm embedded in each tuft
There's a forest moving.
Everybody smiles
and smiles.

III

The crows will never learn
there is garbage enough for everyone:

the mouths of the young are raw red,
soundless.
The egret alights on the topmost branch.
Not a leaf is disturbed.
On all sides the ocean.

IV
Stretch marks of the city
Look the other way:
there are dhows there
Arab horses for desert kingdoms
An old monkey coughs in a tree
The young sense food
jump from rock to burning rock
We bar doors and windows
cower, nursing warm beer
An eagle hovers on a branch split
by lightning.

Otherness/Wise

I have spoken much of
otherness
and must now, alas,
practice what I teach.
Your poems are no longer
messages for me
and mine have become
an epitaph
for a late November afternoon
when the last rays touched
the leaves, the brass, the old teak chest,
and I forgot for a while
what an old painter friend taught me:
Forms without ache, he said, are futile.
So be it. Though I would have it
otherwise.

It's Time to Find a Place

It's time to find a place
to be silent with each other.
I have prattled endlessly
in staff-rooms, corridors, restaurants.
When you're not around
I carry on conversations in my head.
Even this poem
has forty-eight words too many.

Outside Jaisalmer

I

The sea receded. The dunes remember.
Trees have turned quietly to stone.
I watch two men bend intently
over a pawnbroker's scales
and think of you:
Walled city. Dead kings.
The tarred road melts where we stand.

II

Sixty miles from the border
stories:
the general on the other side
doesn't want war, he wants to
cultivate his poppy fields.
We're here to watch the sun set.
Birds fly in formation, and jets.

III

The life of the hero on the scabbard of a sword.
Faces in profile, erect penis in profile,
the colours raw, the rug in detail.
The milk he's washed in has turned a little sour.

Her hand touches her veil.
He looks into her eyes
she looks into his.
Behind the lattice work the waiting women
cry oh and stroke their breasts.

IV
We clatter over five river beds
broad, sweeping, dry
tour potters' weavers' villages
and Kuldera, deserted in protest
against a greedy king.
An old man brings out a few fossils
and says, Once there was a sea
(a hundred and eighty million years ago
but he doesn't know that).
The children say Hello
and look at my shoes.

From *Dangerlok* (2001)

Pahari Parrots

I

Not for him the cold swathes
of pine and mist,
hook-nosed king of a succulent sky.
In his wire-mesh cage
He gives nothing away.
I buy him on impulse.
He makes my flat his home:
Rubber plants, candles, pencils, plastic
make a fine confetti . . .
Princely wastrel of a
lost kingdom.

II

She peers through lattice windows
at the empty street
the long afternoon broken
only by the squawks of parrots.
The air is humid
but there is no rain.

III

Sometimes we compare notes:
I talk about the parrots
She talks about her children.
She tells me little K cries for effect.
If I get home after dark, I tell her,
they look at me with sad, reproachful eyes.
At dusk, all three of us and
all three of them
are melancholic.
Both want to sit on her lap.
Both want to sit on my left shoulder.
I smoke and down a vodka.
Soon I'll be a whiskery old lady
mumbling in my gums
hobbling about
two parrots in my hair.

IV

At the sight of Campari the parrots make
little weak-kneed noises.
Toth pulls the glass one way
Tothi the other
both hang on when I pull.
It's a regular bar-room brawl.

V

Spring, and the trees are translucent.
One can hardly tell
leaf from parrot
berries from beak
red splash on wing
from veins that tingle.

VI

Two trees and a garbage heap.
The garbage brings the barbets.
The parrots love the peepul tree.
There's a bulbul singing in the ashoka.
Throw in sparrows, crows and mynahs
you have your common city garden
complete with pandemonium at dawn.
The lady on the third floor says
We should cut down the trees
she can't sleep for the noise.
Lady, you're a fingernail
scratching a blackboard.

Poems (2002–09)

Mid-Sentence

You left mid-sentence—
Exam House, you said, that degree certificate . . .
I watched you turn the corner of the house, wave,
say you'd ring Sunday.
That was it.
Finis. Kaput. Dead.
Where you are there's neither harp nor halo
nor, what you preferred, an endless ashen dawn
beyond the reach of the sun.
It was thoughtless to vanish so suddenly.

My Mother Feared Death

I
My mother feared death,
hated black, and
doors, grilles, locks
that would not open.
Coffins, crematoriums.
No way to treat a lady.

II
Monsoon burials are a problem.
Coffins float up. Mourners slither
and slide on mounds of muck.
Habits die hard.
I'll phone her, give her the details, I think,
as I look at her with her eyes closed
and her mouth sealed with cotton.

III
My neighbour wants to know
what is to happen to my dead aunt's clothes,
so many of them new, her gold.
Who gets the pickings?
What colour was the coffin?

Death was not fastidious either.
It wrenched the intestines
riveted her eyes
locked her fingers over borrowed beads.
No, life's not cheap here.
Just unsubtle.

IV
Alive or dead, mothers are troubling.
Mine came back and said, 'I'm lonely.'
I left the windows open and the lights on.
She was buried in blue.
It remained. Nothing else did.
Handed back to us in a plastic bag
her bones are forced into a niche.
'I'm lonely,' she says.
I dream of her.
It's the best I can do.

Travelling

I

We walk to the shrine of the diamond-eyed god
This is the hour he's in green and gold
The women moan
He looks a little camp to me
upturned palm with rose
joss sticks burning
but oh those black granite thighs

II

Green roses on a terrace
lemon grass, a golden moon
a golden oriole chases a crow
Mine host waxeth sentimental.
Not a lover in sight.

III

The tattered balladeers invoke the
sun, the moon, the stars,
sing of kings who rode a night of sand
to plant a flag
on yet another sand dune,
of women who died when the sands shifted

in the wind.
A bulbul sings in the thorn tree.

IV
Wedged between houses, a sliver of sea,
casuarinas, clean sand,
infinity.

V
This town boasts a one-armed postal clerk
always drunk
a dog named Dumpy who can't stand the smell of drink
a street with three war widows and two light-eyed girls
who went astray
seven hen-pecked husbands
Copernicus who likes to treat his friends
and disappear when the bill appears . . .
Never underestimate a dishevelled town
the colonel says
reaching for the rum.

Sacred River

Two logs fastened in the river
for birds to take the waters
I saw no birds there
just a cremation or two on the ghats
onlookers at a safe distance
yet another pregnant half-starved stray dog
a white man playing at being a sadhu
top knot and all
But nothing stops faith
No. Nothing stops faith.
It will be heaven to get out of here.

Tothi

Tothi's back
Her beak slightly battered
Her panache intact.
She whistles for me from outside the grille.
I rush with offerings
of guava and melon.

Aunt

My aunt loves bright colours.
Widowhood be damned.
Ninety-one years be damned.
She reads the newspapers from
first page to last
looking for a cheerful story.

Koel 1

Koel, stop those cries.
I can't take it this morning.
The wood-doves join your chorus of grief.
Look! The leaves are shining green
the sky a sort of blue
there's even a breeze from the sea.
We'll survive somehow,
Koel, stop those cries.

Invitation

She tempts me with a vision of hills
grass that's green
peacocks as common as sparrows
We can read in the courtyard, she says,
to the sound of the woodpecker working his tree,
admire her roses, pluck fruit, count stars.
Bring aunt, dogs, parakeet, she says,
write a happy poem or two.
Once in a way, she says,
we'll take a little walk to the village
to find out how the world's
not getting on.

Death

Under the dusty mango tree
ceremonial shaving of heads.
The newly bald make fun of each other.
The newly dead is an unknown quantity
urged on by the tuneless singing of the women,
and men in white standing their ground.

To a Naturalist

Mine's an humbler occupation,
hunting dog ticks, bed bugs, ants
whose steadfastness I can rarely match.
Fed up of concrete, a rat decided to
take up residence in my oven.
Watchman and broom soon settled him.
The wild parakeets chortle their way
through the seed box, three times a day.
As for the fat pigeons
pushing each other off my air conditioner,
there's no escape from their
orgasmic cries.

Learn from the
Almond Leaf (2016)

Learn from the Almond Leaf

Learn from the almond leaf
which flames as it falls.
The ground is burning.
The earth is burning.
Flamboyance
is all.

I Disentangled the Moon

I disentangled the moon
from the branches.
It's disappeared.
I built a house.
Sparrows no longer frolic
in the mud.
I chopped down the tree
that obstructed my view.
A lone raven breaks into song.

Kite Season

The trees are festooned with kites
of many colours.
The trees are festooned with birds
hanging by a wing
an entangled leg
glass-coated string.

Summer

Ash pits all across the land.
In some, the fires of Holi
still smoulder.
Even the moon has begun
to take refuge from the sun.

Close on the Heels

Close on the heels
of a hot October
comes a hot November
a hot December.
Somebody up there, down there,
anywhere
have mercy.
You are about to make cinders
of us all.

A Smattering of Rain

A smattering of rain,
Earth lets off steam.
A hawk falls.
A volcano upchucks.
Watch it!
Earth's heart is still
smouldering.

Compound Life

1
The first-floor procuress
takes the air.
Her bosom precedes her.
Ditto the pigeon
that follows her.

2
She has a quacking voice.
He has duck-tailed hair.

3
Mrs P's daughter never smiles
never talks
walks with her head down
looking for potholes and pitfalls.

4
Mrs V beats her husband.
The churchman says:
Into every life
a little rain must fall.

5

What can trees do in such a place
except light their own fires.

6

The night watchman
sleeps through the night.
Opening his tiffin he says
This is a good job.
The best I ever had.

7

A compound full of silver cars.
The sky with not a single silver star.

8

A bird hovers.
A word hovers.
A word is a bird
is a bird is a bird

9

Hot, still, dawn air.
A rat, condemned to gnaw,
the only sound.

10
The downstairs neighbours sing:
Yes
Yes Yes Lord
Yes

Western Ghats

Fling my ashes in the Western Ghats
They've always seemed like home.
May the leopards develop
a taste for poetry
the crows and kites learn
to modulate their voices.
May there be mist and waterfalls
grass and flowers
in the wrong season.

For the Love of Lout, my Dog

For the love of Lout, my dog,
a howling pup abandoned
at my doorstep
I'll wake at four to walk him.
He's a friendly dog,
a sniffer of crotches.
The good ladies of the neighbourhood
avoid him. So do the men.
He knows too many secrets.

Aubade 2

We talk across continents.
It's unlikely we'll meet again.
Can't smoke, can't travel,
and certainly no heaven.
A cold wind at our backs
we abjure philosophy.
Done with errant lovers, husbands,
not quite wise old birds.
We're still the age at which we met.

Makeshift

Makeshift homes for the living
Makeshift the marriage tent
Makeshift the bier
for the final journey
Makeshift the ground
on which we stand.

Mithi River

Friend, come off that parapet.
The Mithi River won't let you
sink or swim.
It will carry you
on a raft of garbage
to a dying sea.
Friend, come down.
Let be.

Mother Crow

Mother runs her beak
against his feathers.
He submits, head bowed.
There! He's ready for the day.
Nest to my window, window to nest.
His mouth is a cavern.
Anything goes.

Baby Parrot

Baby parrot in my seed box
stares at me
as if I were the devil's own.
Who do you think
provides the seeds, buster?
No answer.
He's yet to learn English.
I've yet to learn Parrot.

Drenched Crow

A drenched crow
huddled against the rain
is not a crow.
A crow is a patriarchal caw
a sharp look
a pretence he's not the crow
I fed a minute ago.

Egrets

Elegant in white,
egrets
step across the river
that never moves.
At sundown flock to,
cover a tree.
Snow
in a sunburnt land.

Rat

Rat as road kill.
Roadkill a feast for crows.
Rats are worshipped in some places,
Snakes in others.
Crows, cleaners of cities
are not worshipped at all.

One Tree

One tree makes a garden.
Two trees make a wood,
Three trees make a forest.

Finally

Finally, the Lord said:
Move that damned highrise.
Let there be light.

Reluctant Spring

The golden orioles have gone
The warblers are silent.
The last red leaf on the almond tree
refuses to fall.

Earth 2

Earth is tired.
Her bones creak and grind
against each other.
Flatulent,
She upchucks lava.
No, not a pretty sight.
Have a care, though.
The crone's still capable
of spite.

Tell me

Tell me, Mr Death
Date, Time, Place.
I have to look for my
life-of-sin panties,
make an appointment
for a pedicure.

Yet Another Death Poem

I keep hearing sounds
of wind and water.
There is no wind.
There is no water.
There is no air.
I see the pallor on her face
the hardening hand
I know
there's no one there.

Avocado Stone

I have planted an avocado stone
in my kitchen
for Ruth
and for Alan who died.
Both friends, Ruth more so—
She of the voice of
oatmeal and honey.
I will replant the stone
give it room to be a tree
To last
as long as grief lasts.

Going

You're going, she said
as his coffin was carried
to the grave,
he didn't reply, of course.
He never replied.
Popping peanuts into his mouth
he went through the evening paper.
At breakfast
egg yolk dribbled down his chin.

Koel 2

Koel, damsel fleeing in distress,
filling the sky with sound.
The crows here tell a different story.
You have no monopoly on grief
(or the crows on fury).
Look below you.
The earth is reeling.

Unsaddle the Sun

Unsaddle the sun.
He has nowhere to ride.
Leave the haze on the stars.
They have nothing to see.
Let the moon drift,
the waters rise.
Leave earth bereft.

April

Listen for the small birds
and the leaves' slow unfurling.
Gods crouch in the pipal tree,
pampered, ineffective
drowning the air with bells and raucous worshippers.
Listen for the small birds,
the lone black butterfly
pausing on the jasmine.

Remains

My mother's bones in a niche.
My aunt's ashes likewise.

A lifetime.
A lifetime.

Earth 1

The earth is restless tonight,
beyond our power to assuage.
Our knowledge comes too late.

She is victim, judge and jury.
She is the avenging angel.

Pray that our deaths
be quick and merciful.

The Moon is Feeling Her Age

The moon is feeling her age.
All this waxing and waning.
A long haul
to no purpose.
Even the dogs howl.

Moon

Pummelled out of shape,
out of style, scarred,
the moon hides her face
behind The Towers.
She's in no hurry to emerge:
she has a desert to cross,
and a line of broken hills.

Moon and Star

Moon and star survey the earth
in tandem—
Dogs, cats, sundry mammals.
Moon picks out a poet
staring at her.
Not again, she thinks.
"The moon is feeling her age,"
forsooth!
"Pummeled out of shape,"
indeed!
Moon madness.

Guide to a Well-Behaved Parrot

Damn that book.
Damn that bird.
Another packet of cigs lies in shreds
on the floor.
Show who's boss, the book says.
I shout at him.
He shouts back.
Really, I may as well have been
married.

New Poems (2015–17)

Bulbul

We really must bring bulbuls back
into poetry.
I can set my watch by this one's song.
There he is,
above the tumult of crows
chattering mynahs, loud-voiced humans.
He is pure sound.

Cousin

At my mother's funeral
a cousin swathed in black
stood as far as she could
from the burial site.

I gestured to her:
Come closer.
No, she said, No,
And she ran through the overgrown churchyard
where locals played football.

Well, I don't fancy mud on my face either.

A four-hundred-year-old church.
My meticulous mother.

Flood City

Poems come flooding in,
Rains come pouring in.
We're a drowning city.
People care about
a drowning city.
Poems can go hang.

Staying Put

It's the three female parrots
who flew away.
The male stayed put.
Likes to be waited on
hand and foot.
There's a lesson there
somewhere.

Unpoetic Thoughts

1
Unfinished poem?
What's to finish in a
two-line poem?

2
You are studying poetries?
Darlings, stick with me
no matter what language you speak.

3
A cliché?
Lock him up
and throw the key away.

4
A great fat slimy
African snail
on the outer wall?
UGH!
I always wanted to say
Ugh
in a poem.

5

Ugha. Ugha.
That's Neanderthal.
I'm an open-minded gal.

6
Being ill brings on poetry.
Being well, likewise.
Open season for poets
and poetry

7
I'm not averse
to verse.
I just prefer
poetries.

8
The rains.
Romance is in the air.
That's unfair.
Rain brings me
despair.

9
4 am.
High on words
and vodka.
The words are okay.
The vodka is strident.

10
You're a poet?
Okay.
So I'm a poet.

11
The 4 am vodka bothers you?
Sweetest love
Vodka in a poetrie
is not a vodka

12
Aap potries likhte hai?
Ji.
Hamara beta bhi . . .
Hell and damnation!
Waiter!
Vodka!

13
A two-line poem
and an epic
are both poetries,

Joking or what?

14
Why she talking nonsense?
It's called language, dear.

15
Damn you.
I am NOT a damp squib.

16
Enjoyed?
No.
No?
No.

17
You want real poetries?
Sun, moon, stars, rain
Here we go again

Eternity

A fatuous fate awaits us all.
Eternity.
Eternal, eternal eternity.
The same damn harp music,
the endless fluttering of wings.
Pious looks abound.

I suppose I could stream down
on light from a distant star.
Ride rough in the eye of a storm.

Then what?

Thunderstorm

Thunderbolts.
Lightning flashes.

Relax, folks,
it's just me on my way
to my Heavenly Abode.

Appendix I

Preface to *A Necklace of Skulls* by Eunice de Souza,
2009 edition

I'd like to thank Ravi Singh for suggesting this volume of
collected poems. My books, like those of many other poets,
have not been available for years and readers have had to
depend on anthologies. In any case, *Ways of Belonging*,
which was published by Polygon in Edinburgh, has never
been available in India.

I'd also like to thank the poets' cooperatives which
published my first book *Fix* in 1979 (Arun Kolatkar
designed the cover), and the second, *Women in Dutch
Painting*, in 1988. Santan Rodrigues, Melanie Silgardo and
Raul da Gama Rose formed Newground which published
their own book, *Three Poets*, and several others including
Fix. Adil Jussawalla was in charge of Praxis which published
Women in Dutch Painting. *Ways of Belonging* and *Selected and
New Poems* (Department of English, St Xavier's College,
Mumbai) included many of the poems from the first
two books, but also contained new sections. My novella
Dangerlok, published by Penguin Books India in 2001, also
contains some poems. In the present volume I've included
some early poems, which for reasons I cannot remember

were not published, and some new ones too. The poem 'Alibi' which should have been in *Fix* was left out at the time, mainly because I had this vision of reviewers using one of the phrases from the poem as their title, 'a sour old puss in verse'.

I haven't kept track of exactly when I wrote each poem, but there is one date I do remember—28 August 1971, Adil and Veronik Jussawalla's wedding day. I couldn't be part of their celebrations as I was ill, and it was pouring anyway. But I sent them one of the poems I had just written, a thoroughly unsuitable one—'Marriages Are Made'. I first met Adil in London in the sixties, the same time when I first met Farrukh Dhondy, though he lived down the street from me in Poona, and when I caught up again with Mala Sen, Darryl D'Monte and their circle of friends. Adil and Veronik were endlessly supportive when I lived in a grungy paying-guest room in Colaba.

Earlier, on my return from the US where I did my graduate work, I met Nissim Ezekiel when he interviewed me for a teaching job. He assured me I would be unhappy at the college he represented so I didn't take the job, but was intrigued by his suggestion that we meet at the ticket counter in Churchgate. I had no idea what he looked like, or how he would spot me in the usual mob milling around. Through him I met Gieve Patel, Kamala Das, Dom Moraes and others. I feel privileged to know/to have known all of them.

I wish I could remember more about the days in the seventies when I began writing poetry. A.D. Gorwala of the little magazine *Opinion* published some of the early 'Catholic' poems, as did *Vrischik* which was published in Baroda, and the then new supplement of the *Times of India* accompanied by Mario Miranda's cartoons which, according to a poet friend, unfortunately took some of the bite out of the poems. In the mid-seventies Melanie Silgardo, who was at St Xavier's, Mumbai, and I organized readings at which both established and newer poets read their work.

At a conference in Delhi, the Australian poet A.D. Hope asked me to send him whatever I had written (I hadn't published a book yet), and wrote me a morale-boosting letter about the poems. I needed that boost because at the same conference a Canadian academic told me that my poems weren't really poems because they didn't have images. This worried me because I was already unsure of the rather jagged pieces I had produced when all I wanted to write were lyrical poems with soft, sensuous and passionate lines! Regardless of what I told my students, only lyrical poetry seemed like 'real' poetry to me. Even when Adil Jussawalla said that the poems themselves were images, fixing people and situations at a 'decisive moment', it took me a long time to be convinced. It wasn't until the second book was published that I began to feel I was a poet.

So I was astonished by the response to the poems in *Fix*, particularly those which expressed ambivalence towards a parent. These responses sometimes came from people who did not always read poetry. This sense of being able to relate to people through my work meant a great deal to me as a person and as a poet.

The creative process being what it is, I don't really know where the poems came from. But I am endlessly grateful that they turned up.

Appendix II

Foreword to *A Necklace of Skulls* by Melanie Silgardo,
2019 edition

When Eunice de Souza died in July 2017, she left little
that required tidying up or sorting out. She had organized
her papers—letters, reviews, certificates, ephemera—neatly
into folders, photos into albums; had given away to friends
things precious to her: pictures, paintings, furniture. Her last
volume of poetry had been published the year before with
urgency. Fiercely independent to the last, despite her failing
health, she had got herself into a state of preparedness. *Learn
from the Almond Leaf*, a slim, elegiac volume full of agonizing
presentiment ('Tell me, Mr Death / Date. Time. Place.';
'Earth is tired / Her bones creak and grind') was a tying
up of loose ends, a saying of goodbye. This collection, *A
Necklace of Skulls*, predating it by several years, is a collection
of her complete earlier poems, including her pioneering
first book of poems, *Fix*.

To write this foreword to *A Necklace of Skulls*, which
Penguin are reissuing, is a great personal privilege. For
me, Eunice's death marked not just the end of a lifelong
friendship, but the end of an institution that was Eunice de
Souza. I had known her for more than forty years, first as

a student, then publisher and friend. When we published *Fix* in 1979, we knew we were putting into print a volume of poetry that was quite different from anything around. Eunice, though, felt unsure of the poems, wondered whether they were poems at all. Validation came from some of her closest contemporaries and friends. For Adil Jussawalla, writing on the cover of *Fix*, the poems had 'an accuracy of detail and something of the quality of photographs taken at a decisive moment'; for Arvind Krishna Mehrotra, writing in the introduction to her poems in *Twelve Indian Poets*, they had 'the brevity, unexpectedness and urgency of telegrams'.

Fix was first published in 1979 by Newground. Clearing House had scheduled it for their next batch but Eunice was impatient; the manuscript had been lying around too long and she wanted it out there. Santan Rodrigues, Raul da Gama Rose and I had just published *Three Poets*, ourselves, in Newground's first ever volume. It was based on the Clearing House model and was a success. When I suggested to Eunice that we might publish her her response was immediate and unequivocal. Arun Kolatkar's cover design for *Fix* was magnificent—stark and bold—an almost life-size portrait of Eunice in silvered black and white, cropped close around the head, her gaze direct, unflinching, her forehead marked with a cross or an X, calling to mind the iconography of mug shots, of prisoners about to do time. It was a groundbreaking volume of poems—original, punchy, daring, seething with rage, undercut with self-irony. From the very first poem, 'Catholic Mother', she was to establish her poetic DNA as she excoriated hypocrisy and pretension, whether in the community, family or relationships.

> We've had seven children
> (in seven years)
> [. . .]
> Pillar of the Church
> says the parish priest
> Lovely Catholic Family
> says Mother Superior
> the pillar's wife
> says nothing.

These were poems that didn't just pick and prod at the Goan Catholic community, but were nuanced with the registers of sympathy ('Miss Louise') and irony ('Conversation Piece'), and had rippling underneath a dark and visceral vision and a deeply emotional literacy ('Forgive Me, Mother'). Self-awareness, guilt, forgiveness and reparation were to be recurring themes:

> Poems can have order, sanity,
> aesthetic distance from the debris,
> All I've learnt from pain

I always knew,
but could not do.
('Don't Look for My Life in These Poems')

She never baulked at using her life, her curiosity, her engagement with lovers, friends, students, retainers as her material. But her poems transcended the personal, the 'confessional'—she gave them context and moral perspective with a lightness, dryness, irreverence and humour that became her hallmark. She always maintained she never set out to write like this, she just did: 'Just keep at what you are:/ a sour old puss in verse/ and leave the rest to me.'

A Necklace of Skulls charts her transition from *Fix*, through to her later volumes—*Women in Dutch Painting* and *Ways of Belonging*—and poems unpublished in any of these volumes. For a writing life spanning more than forty years her output was lean, pared-down. Every word and every line was turned over, inspected for the superfluous ('Even this poem/has forty-eight words too many' ['It's Time to Find a Place']). That was how she wrote. Even when she was working on her weekly column for the *Mumbai Mirror* in the days before, she would sit in front of her laptop and would be what she always called 'mulling', waiting for the ideas, the intersections, the connections, the clarity. In her final volume *Learn from the Almond Leaf* (Poetrywala 2016), she delighted in saying the poems came in the wee hours of the morning when her restless dog would drag her out of bed for a walk in the compound, when the not-yet dawn and unusual quiet of her bustling neighbourhood forged whole poems in her head that she hastily dashed down in an exercise book.

She honed and whittled till she got to the nub of things. Her language was always precise, her cadence colloquial, her punctuation minimal, her ear exact. She used the voice and persona to great effect and she was master of the nuanced line. She often quoted Robert Browning's poem *My Last Duchess* as having a lasting influence on her. She admired the scope of the dramatic monologue, the changes in tone and voice, the suggestion and the loaded yet unsaid statement—all elements she would come to use herself. Unlike Browning, she used form and structure casually but with just as deadly effect.

The death of her father when she was three haunted her throughout her life. It was a loss she never really recovered from and many of her poems are charged with symbols and recurring images referencing this loss—monsoons, mists, blue hills—a chilling pull towards oblivion and then the coming up for air—as in:

It's too late for me
to die young
as you did

[. . .] I cling to little things—
a glossy new leaf
a singing bird at dawn
[. . .] I convince myself
[. . .] that living does not desecrate
your memory. ('Untitled')

or

You are the cold wind
The grey mist.
The black dawn.
The grinning skull.
I am you. ('For My Father, Dead Young')

She writes about childhood with a piercing nostalgia: 'In school/ I clutched Sister Flora's skirt/ and cried for my mother/ who taught across the road/ Sister Flora is dead/ The school is still standing/ I am still learning/ to cross the road' ('The Road (for Deepak Ananth)'). The issues of belonging, difference and abandonment permeate her poems. From the wider cultural context to the more personal ('I've heard it said/ my parents wanted a boy' ['de Souza Prabhu']) her vein of feminism runs all the way through—even scolding Tukaram: 'You made life hard for your wife/ and I'm not sure I approve of that' ['Return'].

In *Women in Dutch Painting* and *Ways of Belonging* she moves into a more introspective space, but no less challenging. She circles the self, offers advice peppered with the right amount of wit and spite ('Keep cats/ if you want to learn to cope with/ the otherness of lovers'), writes love poems that bite ('I choose not to marry you, love./ There is poison in my tongue'). Then there are poems such as 'Songs of Innocence', one of my favourites, where she casts her net wide from banal kindergarten Bible study to the deeply moving foraging for ancestral roots to establish a sense of belonging. In the poem 'Notations' in *Ways of Belonging* she harks back to an oral tradition where less is more and where loss permeates everything: 'It happened: that is all they say. It happened.' She saw the Bhakti poets, Tukaram in particular, and the women poets in general as her literary ancestors. Like them she could write about the minutiae of daily life and the vastness of the universe in the space of a few lines ('So you are going too, my love,/ the last, most beautiful/ of my children/ [. . .] One sets them free—/ to learn, finally learn/ to claim nothing'). She was a poet whose touchstone was the honest, the authentic, the unguarded self. She left us a small but potent legacy— poems that will survive us all.

Scan QR code to access the
Penguin Random House India website